TABLE OF CONTENTS

Microsoft Sway

The Microsoft 365 Companion Series

Dr. Patrick Jones

OLYMPUS ACADEMY
PRESS

CREATIVITY MEETS SIMPLICITY

In a world where effective communication is more important than ever, the way we present information can make all the difference. Whether you're sharing a personal story, delivering a professional report, or crafting a visual presentation, your tools should work with you, not against you. Enter Microsoft Sway, a dynamic and intuitive app that transforms how you communicate through visually engaging, interactive content.

But what makes Sway so unique? Unlike traditional tools like PowerPoint or Word, Sway focuses on simplicity and design, allowing you to create polished, modern presentations, newsletters, reports, and more without needing advanced graphic design skills. With its effortless drag-and-drop interface and smart design suggestions, Sway empowers anyone—from students to professionals—to communicate ideas in a way that's both impactful and accessible.

Imagine needing to present a complex concept to your team or share a memorable travel story with friends. Traditional slides might feel too rigid, and word documents might not capture the visual essence of your message. This is where Sway excels, bridging the gap between content and creativity.

With Sway, you don't need to worry about layout or formatting—it takes care of the design so you can focus on the story you want to tell. Whether your audience is a room of executives or a classroom full of students, Sway's interactive and visually appealing presentations ensure your message stands out.

Example: Sarah, a marketing manager, used Sway to create a sleek and interactive project report for her team. The polished design not only impressed her audience but also made complex data easier to digest.

This book is your companion to mastering Microsoft Sway, offering a step-by-step journey into understanding, using, and maximizing this innovative tool. Whether you're just starting or want to refine your skills, each chapter is designed to build your confidence and creativity. Here's what you can expect:

1. **What Is Microsoft Sway?** Discover Sway's unique features and how it fits into the Microsoft 365 ecosystem.

2. **Why Use Sway?** Learn the benefits of Sway and explore real-world scenarios where it can transform your communication.

3. **Getting Started:** Step-by-step guidance on setting up your first Sway, from adding content to choosing layouts.

4. **Best Practices:** Tips for creating visually compelling and audience-focused Sways.

5. **Tips and Tricks:** Uncover hidden features and shortcuts that can save time and elevate your designs.

6. **Common Pitfalls:** Avoid common mistakes and learn how to troubleshoot effectively.

7. **Episode:** Follow Sarah's journey as she discovers the power of Sway for her professional and personal projects.

8. **Summary and Reflection:** Recap the key lessons and reflect on how Sway can transform your own workflows.

9. **Final Thoughts:** Explore how Sway fits into the broader Microsoft 365 ecosystem and how your journey doesn't stop here.

This isn't just a technical manual—it's a conversational guide designed to make learning enjoyable and accessible. Through relatable stories, practical examples, and actionable tips, you'll feel like you have a guide on the side, helping you every step of the way.

As you progress, you'll not only master Sway but also gain a deeper understanding of how to communicate more effectively in today's digital world.

Let's dive in and explore how Microsoft Sway can unlock your creativity and transform the way you share ideas. Your journey to effortless, impactful communication starts here!

WHAT IS MICROSOFT SWAY?

Microsoft Sway is a modern, intuitive tool designed to help you create visually stunning and interactive presentations, reports, newsletters, and more. Unlike traditional presentation tools like PowerPoint, Sway simplifies the design process, allowing you to focus on your content while it handles layout and formatting. With its drag-and-drop interface, seamless integration with other Microsoft 365 apps, and smart design suggestions, Sway empowers users of all skill levels to communicate ideas in a creative and engaging way.

But Sway isn't just about presentations—it's a versatile tool that adapts to a wide variety of uses, from professional projects to personal storytelling. Whether you're a student, teacher, business professional, or creative enthusiast, Sway offers a unique way to transform your ideas into shareable, polished narratives.

At first glance, Sway might seem similar to PowerPoint or Word, but it serves a distinct purpose within the Microsoft 365 suite. While PowerPoint focuses on slide-based presentations and Word on text-heavy documents, Sway bridges the gap by offering:

- **A Storytelling Approach:** Instead of static slides, Sway creates a fluid, scrollable format that guides your audience through a cohesive narrative.

- **Simplified Design:** You don't need graphic design expertise—Sway's intelligent layout engine takes care of visual elements, ensuring professional results.

- **Interactivity:** Embed videos, images, charts, and even interactive web content to engage your audience.

Example: Melissa, a teacher, used Sway to create an interactive lesson plan for her students, combining text, videos, and quizzes. The result was more engaging and visually appealing than a traditional document.

Core Features of Sway

1. **Effortless Design**

   o Sway's design engine automatically adjusts layouts to create a polished, cohesive look.

   o Choose from professionally designed templates or let Sway suggest layouts based on your content.

   o Customize colors, fonts, and styles with just a few clicks.

Pro Tip: If you're unsure where to start, Sway's "Remix" button generates random design suggestions to spark inspiration.

2. **Content Integration**

   o Drag and drop text, images, videos, and files directly into Sway.

   o Connect to OneDrive, YouTube, or your device to pull in content seamlessly.

   o Use Sway's built-in Bing search to find copyright-friendly images and videos.

Example: Sarah included high-quality images from Bing's Creative Commons search in her Sway presentation, elevating its visual impact.

3. **Interactive Elements**

   o Embed dynamic content like tweets, polls, charts, or even 3D models.

   o Add interactive navigation features to make your Sway presentations user-friendly.

Pro Tip: Use interactive elements to keep your audience engaged during presentations or reports.

4. **Cross-Device Compatibility**

   o Sway is cloud-based, meaning your projects are accessible from any device with an internet connection.

   o Projects automatically adjust to fit different screen sizes, ensuring a consistent experience on desktops, tablets, and smartphones.

Example: Sarah shared her Sway newsletter with clients, who viewed it seamlessly on their phones during a commute.

5. **Sharing Made Simple**

   o Share your Sway projects with a single link—no bulky files or attachments.

   o Control access levels (public, organization-only, or specific recipients).

   o Embed your Sway into websites or blogs for greater reach.

One of Sway's strengths is its integration with the Microsoft 365 suite. It works seamlessly with tools like:

- **Word and OneNote:** Import text and notes directly into Sway to create cohesive presentations.

- **PowerPoint:** Transform slide decks into dynamic Sway presentations with added interactivity.

- **OneDrive:** Access and embed files stored in the cloud.

Example: Sarah used OneNote to draft her ideas, then imported the content into Sway for a visually compelling final project.

Sway's versatility makes it suitable for a wide range of projects, including:

- **Business Reports:** Share insights with stakeholders through interactive charts and visuals.

- **Educational Materials:** Create engaging lesson plans, study guides, or classroom newsletters.

- **Personal Projects:** Build digital scrapbooks, event invitations, or travel journals.

- **Marketing Content:** Design sleek newsletters, product demos, or promotional presentations.

Pro Tip: Explore Sway's templates to jumpstart your creativity, whether you're designing a company profile or a family photo album.

Sway's combination of simplicity and sophistication has made it a favorite among users looking for a tool that balances creativity with ease of use. Here's why users love it:

- **No Learning Curve:** Its intuitive interface means you can start creating immediately, even if you're not tech-savvy.

- **Professional Results:** Sway's smart design ensures your projects always look polished.

- **Collaboration-Friendly:** Share and edit projects with colleagues or friends in real time.

Now that you understand what Sway is and how it fits into the Microsoft 365 ecosystem, it's time to explore why you should consider using it for your projects.

WHY USE MICROSOFT SWAY?

In today's fast-paced, visually driven world, how you present information matters just as much as the information itself. Microsoft Sway isn't just another tool—it's a game-changer for anyone looking to create engaging, interactive, and professional presentations with minimal effort. Whether you're a student, educator, professional, or creative, Sway offers a unique blend of simplicity and sophistication that makes it an essential tool in the Microsoft 365 suite.

In this chapter, we'll explore the key reasons to use Sway, from its ease of use and time-saving features to its ability to create stunning, immersive presentations that capture attention and leave a lasting impression.

1. Effortless Creativity Without the Design Skills

Sway takes the pressure out of creating visually appealing presentations by handling the design for you. Its intelligent design engine ensures your content looks polished and professional, even if you don't have a background in graphic design.

- **Pre-Designed Templates:** Start with a template and let Sway guide you, or customize the layout to match your vision.

- **Automatic Adjustments:** Sway's dynamic layout adapts to fit your content, ensuring consistency and balance.

- **Custom Branding:** Adjust colors, fonts, and styles to align with your personal or organizational branding.

Example: Sarah, a small business owner, needed to create a marketing pitch. With Sway's intuitive tools, she built a stunning presentation in under an hour—no design experience required.

Pro Tip: Use the "Remix" button for instant design inspiration and a fresh perspective on your content.

2. Interactive and Engaging Presentations

One of Sway's standout features is its ability to incorporate interactivity, transforming static presentations into immersive experiences.

- **Embed Multimedia:** Add videos, images, and even live web content to bring your ideas to life.

- **Interactive Navigation:** Let viewers scroll through your presentation at their own pace, enhancing engagement.

- **Dynamic Elements:** Use animations and transitions to make your content more engaging without overwhelming your audience.

Example: Sarah created a project proposal with embedded videos and interactive charts, impressing her stakeholders and securing their buy-in.

Pro Tip: Include quizzes or polls in educational Sways to encourage participation and feedback.

3. Seamless Sharing and Collaboration

Sway simplifies sharing by allowing you to distribute your content as a link, eliminating the need for bulky attachments or special software.

- **Share Anywhere:** Send a link via email, embed Sway on a website, or share it on social media.

- **Control Access:** Choose who can view or edit your Sway, with options for public, organizational, or specific recipient access.

- **Real-Time Collaboration:** Work with teammates to create or edit a Sway together, no matter where they are.

Example: Sarah shared her company newsletter with clients by embedding the Sway in her website, reaching a broader audience without any technical hurdles.

4. Adaptability Across Use Cases

Sway's versatility makes it suitable for a wide range of applications, from personal projects to professional reports.

- **For Professionals:** Create polished business reports, product demos, or marketing materials.

- **For Educators:** Design interactive lesson plans, study guides, or classroom newsletters.

- **For Students:** Present research projects or creative assignments with a professional edge.

- **For Creatives:** Build visually compelling portfolios, travel journals, or digital scrapbooks.

Example: Sarah, who also teaches part-time, created an engaging digital syllabus for her class using Sway, incorporating videos and links to resources.

Pro Tip: Use Sway's built-in analytics to track engagement, helping you understand how your audience interacts with your content.

5. Accessibility and Cross-Device Compatibility

Sway is cloud-based, meaning you can access and present your content from any device with an internet connection.

- **Device Agnostic:** Your Sway projects look great on desktops, tablets, and smartphones, with layouts automatically adjusting for the best viewing experience.

- **No Software Required:** Viewers don't need special software or accounts to access your Sway—they just click a link.

Example: Sarah presented her Sway marketing pitch to clients using her smartphone, showcasing its flexibility and professionalism.

Pro Tip: Test your Sway on multiple devices before sharing to ensure a seamless experience for your audience.

6. Save Time Without Sacrificing Quality

Creating content can be time-consuming, but Sway's user-friendly interface and intelligent design features streamline the process.

- **Drag-and-Drop Simplicity:** Add content by dragging it directly into Sway, saving time on formatting.

- **Integrated Content Sources:** Pull images, videos, and files directly from your device, OneDrive, or Bing.

- **Smart Suggestions:** Sway offers design and content ideas to enhance your project.

Example: Sarah used Sway to create a polished annual report in half the time it would've taken with traditional tools.

Pro Tip: Start with Sway's templates to jumpstart your project and focus on refining the content.

7. Integration with Microsoft 365

Sway works seamlessly with the Microsoft 365 ecosystem, enhancing its functionality and utility.

- **Import from Word or PowerPoint:** Transform existing documents into engaging Sway presentations.

- **Embed Content from OneDrive:** Link to cloud-stored files for easy sharing.

- **Collaborate with Teams:** Share Sways in Teams channels for real-time feedback.

Example: Sarah converted her PowerPoint presentation into Sway, adding interactive elements for a more modern and dynamic experience.

Microsoft Sway empowers you to create stunning, interactive content that communicates your ideas clearly and effectively. Whether you're working on a professional project, an educational resource, or a personal story, Sway offers the tools to make your vision a reality.

YOUR FIRST STEPS

Creating with Microsoft Sway is a straightforward and enjoyable experience, designed for users of all skill levels. Whether you're a complete beginner or someone looking to polish your skills, this chapter will guide you through the essential steps to create your first Sway. From setting up your project to customizing its design, you'll learn how to bring your ideas to life in just a few clicks.

Step 1: Accessing Microsoft Sway

To start using Sway, you need access to the app through your Microsoft account.

- **From a Browser:**
    - o Go to sway.office.com and sign in with your Microsoft account.
    - o If you're part of an organization, use your work or school account.

Pro Tip: If you're using Microsoft 365, Sway is included with your subscription, so there's no additional cost.

Example: Sarah signed into Sway on her laptop to start her first project and later continued editing it on her tablet during her commute.

Step 2: Creating a New Sway

Once logged in, you're ready to create.

- **Start Fresh:** Click the Create New button to begin with a blank canvas.
- **Use a Template:** Choose from professionally designed templates to get a head start.

- **Import Existing Content:** Upload a Word document or PowerPoint file, and Sway will automatically generate a presentation from your content.

Example: Sarah uploaded a Word document summarizing her marketing plan, letting Sway transform it into an interactive, visually appealing presentation.

Pro Tip: Experiment with templates if you're unsure where to start—they provide a great structure for beginners.

Step 3: Adding Content to Your Sway

Sway's intuitive interface makes adding content simple.

- **Drag and Drop:** Add text, images, videos, and other media by dragging them directly into your Sway.

- **Use the Content Pane:** Click the **+** icon to add specific elements like headings, text, images, or embedded content.

- **Insert from External Sources:** Sway integrates with OneDrive, YouTube, and Bing, allowing you to pull in content without leaving the app.

Example: Sarah added high-quality images from Bing's Creative Commons library and embedded a product demo video from YouTube into her Sway.

Pro Tip: Keep your content concise and visually balanced to maintain audience engagement.

Step 4: Organizing Your Sway

The structure of your Sway plays a crucial role in how your audience experiences it.

- **Sections:** Break your content into logical sections using headings to create a clear narrative flow.

16

- **Reorder Content:** Rearrange elements by dragging and dropping them into the desired sequence.
- **Group Elements:** Combine related content into groups, such as images and captions or multiple charts.

Pro Tip: Use the "Focus Points" feature to emphasize key parts of your images or videos, ensuring your audience sees what matters most.

Step 5: Customizing the Design

Sway's intelligent design engine ensures a polished look, but you can further customize your project.

- **Choose a Theme:** Select from a variety of themes to set the tone and style of your Sway.
- **Adjust Navigation:** Decide whether your audience will scroll vertically, horizontally, or navigate through slides.
- **Use the Remix Button:** Let Sway suggest random design adjustments for inspiration.

Example: Sarah chose a modern theme with horizontal navigation for her marketing pitch, giving it a sleek, professional appearance.

Pro Tip: Preview your Sway before sharing to see how it looks on different devices and screen sizes.

Step 6: Sharing Your Sway

Once your Sway is complete, it's time to share it with your audience.

- **Generate a Shareable Link:** Copy a link to your Sway and share it via email, social media, or messaging apps.
- **Control Access:** Set permissions for public access, organization-only access, or specific recipients.

- **Embed Your Sway:** Add your presentation to a website, blog, or intranet for wider visibility.

Pro Tip: Use analytics (available in organizational accounts) to track how your audience interacts with your Sway, gaining insights into its impact.

Example: Sarah embedded her Sway presentation into her company's intranet, making it accessible to her entire team with a single click.

Step 7: Iterating and Improving

Creating your first Sway is just the beginning. As you become more comfortable with the tool, you'll discover new ways to refine and enhance your projects.

- **Seek Feedback:** Share your Sway with colleagues or friends and ask for their input.

- **Experiment with Features:** Try adding interactive elements like charts, polls, or 3D models to elevate your content.

- **Stay Updated:** Microsoft frequently updates Sway with new features, so keep an eye on what's available.

Pro Tip: Save multiple versions of your Sway to experiment with different designs or narratives without losing your original work.

Now that you've created your first Sway, you're well on your way to mastering this versatile tool.

BEST PRACTICES FOR USING MICROSOFT SWAY

Creating a Sway is easy, but making it effective and engaging requires thoughtful planning and design. In this chapter, we'll dive into best practices for crafting Sway presentations that captivate your audience, deliver clear messages, and stand out for all the right reasons. Whether you're designing a report, a lesson plan, or a personal project, these strategies will help you take your Sway to the next level.

1. Start with a Clear Purpose

Why It Matters:
Before you begin, define the goal of your Sway. Are you informing, persuading, teaching, or entertaining? Understanding your purpose will guide your content and design choices.

Best Practice:

- Outline your key message and supporting points before adding content.
- Keep your audience in mind—what do they need to know, and what's the best way to communicate it?

Example: Sarah created a Sway to pitch a new marketing strategy. She structured her content around three main points: the challenge, the proposed solution, and the expected results.

Pro Tip: Draft a rough outline or storyboard to map out your ideas before diving into Sway.

2. Use Visuals to Enhance, Not Overwhelm

Why It Matters:
Sway's strength lies in its ability to incorporate rich visuals, but too many images or videos can distract from your message.

Best Practice:

- Choose high-quality images and videos that directly support your content.

- Use the Focus Points feature to highlight the most important parts of your visuals.

- Avoid clutter—leave white space to let your content breathe.

Example: Sarah included a graph to illustrate her team's progress and used the Focus Points tool to emphasize key data points.

Pro Tip: Use Sway's built-in Bing search to find royalty-free images and videos that align with your message.

3. Break Content into Manageable Sections

Why It Matters:
Long blocks of text can overwhelm readers. Breaking content into smaller sections makes it easier to digest.

Best Practice:

- Use headings to divide your Sway into clear sections.

- Group related elements, such as images and text, to create cohesive units.

- Limit text to short paragraphs or bullet points for readability.

Example: Sarah divided her Sway into sections like "Overview," "Goals," and "Action Plan," making it easy for her audience to follow along.

Pro Tip: Preview your Sway to ensure each section flows naturally into the next.

4. Choose a Layout That Matches Your Story

Why It Matters:
Sway offers multiple navigation options, and the right choice depends on your content and audience.

Best Practice:

- **Vertical Scrolling:** Great for linear narratives like reports or timelines.
- **Horizontal Scrolling:** Ideal for visually driven content or storytelling.
- **Slide Navigation:** Suitable for traditional presentation styles.

Example: Sarah chose horizontal scrolling for her marketing pitch, creating a sleek, modern feel that matched her brand.

Pro Tip: Experiment with different layouts using the Remix button to find the one that works best for your content.

5. Keep It Interactive

Why It Matters:
Interactive elements like videos, charts, and links make your Sway more engaging and memorable.

Best Practice:

- Embed videos, polls, or 3D models to make your presentation dynamic.
- Use clickable links to direct your audience to additional resources.
- Add animations sparingly to highlight key points without overwhelming viewers.

Example: Sarah embedded a short video demonstration in her Sway, capturing her audience's attention and reinforcing her message.

Pro Tip: Test interactive elements on multiple devices to ensure they work seamlessly for all viewers.

6. Simplify Your Message

Why It Matters:
A concise message is easier for your audience to understand and remember.

Best Practice:

- Focus on one idea per section.

- Use visuals to complement—not repeat—your text.

- Edit ruthlessly to remove unnecessary information.

Example: Sarah used a single, compelling chart to summarize her data instead of cluttering her Sway with multiple graphs.

Pro Tip: Ask a colleague to review your Sway and provide feedback on clarity and focus.

7. Use Branding to Strengthen Identity

Why It Matters:
Consistent branding makes your Sway look professional and reinforces your message.

Best Practice:

- Choose colors and fonts that align with your brand or theme.

- Use a logo or watermark to personalize your Sway.

- Maintain visual consistency throughout the presentation.

Example: Sarah customized her Sway with her company's brand colors and logo, ensuring it matched her other marketing materials.

Pro Tip: Use Sway's theme options to quickly apply a cohesive design across your project.

8. Preview and Test Your Sway

Why It Matters:
What looks great on your screen might not translate perfectly to other devices or audiences.

Best Practice:

- Preview your Sway on desktop, tablet, and smartphone to ensure compatibility.

- Test navigation and interactive elements to confirm they work as intended.

- Check spelling, grammar, and alignment to maintain professionalism.

Example: Sarah previewed her Sway on her phone and adjusted the image sizes to improve readability.

Pro Tip: Share your Sway with a small test audience before presenting it to a larger group.

By following these best practices, you'll create Sways that are not only visually appealing but also effective in delivering your message.

TIPS AND TRICKS FOR MICROSOFT SWAY

Microsoft Sway is already designed to make creating visually stunning and interactive presentations easy, but there are always ways to take your projects to the next level. In this chapter, we'll explore some of the lesser-known features, clever hacks, and time-saving techniques that can help you create Sways that stand out. Whether you're a beginner or a seasoned user, these tips and tricks will elevate your Sway experience.

1. Use the Remix Button for Inspiration

The Trick: Let Sway's design engine surprise you with fresh layout ideas.

- **How It Works:**
    - Click the Remix button at the top of your Sway.
    - Sway will automatically rearrange your content and apply new styles, colors, and fonts.

Pro Tip: If you're stuck on design, use the Remix button multiple times until you find a layout that sparks your creativity.

Example: Sarah used Remix to test different designs for her team presentation, eventually landing on a polished layout she loved.

2. Highlight Key Visuals with Focus Points

The Trick: Draw attention to specific parts of your images.

- **How It Works:**
    - Select an image in your Sway.
    - Click Focus Points and adjust the markers to emphasize the most important areas.

Pro Tip: Use this feature to ensure your audience notices critical details in charts, diagrams, or photographs.

Example: Sarah used Focus Points to highlight her company's logo in a promotional Sway, ensuring it stood out.

3. Leverage Built-In Content Search

The Trick: Quickly find high-quality media without leaving Sway.

- **How It Works:**
    - Use the Insert Content pane to search Bing for images, videos, and more.
    - Filter results to find Creative Commons-licensed content for worry-free use.

Pro Tip: Use specific search terms like "infographic" or "animated video" to find dynamic content that enhances your Sway.

Example: Sarah added professional-looking stock images from Bing's Creative Commons search to make her Sway visually appealing.

4. Group Content for a Cohesive Look

The Trick: Combine related elements into groups to create a unified design.

- **How It Works:**
    - Select multiple elements (e.g., text and an image).
    - Click Group and choose from layouts like stack, grid, or comparison.

Pro Tip: Use the stack layout for step-by-step processes or the comparison layout to highlight differences between two items.

Example: Sarah grouped an infographic and a descriptive paragraph, creating a clean and organized layout for her marketing proposal.

5. Embed External Content for Interactivity

The Trick: Make your Sway dynamic by embedding live content.

- **How It Works:**

    o   Click **+** and select Embed to insert videos, tweets, polls, or other web-based content.

    o   Paste the embed code into the dialog box.

Pro Tip: Use polls or quizzes to engage your audience in real time, especially for educational or marketing Sways.

Example: Sarah embedded a YouTube video tutorial in her Sway, making it an interactive learning resource for her clients.

6. Customize Navigation for Audience Preferences

The Trick: Choose the right navigation style for your content.

- **How It Works:**

    o   Click Design > Navigation and choose Vertical, Horizontal, or Slides.

Pro Tip: Use vertical navigation for reports, horizontal for visual storytelling, and slides for traditional presentations.

Example: Sarah used horizontal navigation for her travel journal Sway, creating a magazine-like browsing experience.

7. Optimize for Mobile Viewing

The Trick: Ensure your Sway looks great on all devices.

- **How It Works:**

    o   Click Play to preview your Sway.

o   Adjust text size, image placement, and navigation style to enhance mobile readability.

Pro Tip: Keep text concise and use larger visuals for better impact on smaller screens.

Example: Sarah previewed her Sway on her smartphone and resized images to ensure they displayed correctly.

8. Save Time with Templates

The Trick: Start with a pre-designed template for faster project creation.

- **How It Works:**

    o   Browse Sway's library of templates for reports, newsletters, portfolios, and more.

    o   Customize the template to suit your needs.

Pro Tip: Templates are especially useful for recurring projects like monthly reports or newsletters.

Example: Sarah used a newsletter template to create a professional client update in minutes.

9. Add Background Music for Atmosphere

The Trick: Set the tone with subtle background music.

- **How It Works:**

    o   Click + > Audio and select a track from your device or external source.

Pro Tip: Choose instrumental music that complements your presentation without distracting from the content.

Example: Sarah added soft instrumental music to her company event recap Sway, creating an immersive experience for viewers.

10. Collaborate in Real Time

The Trick: Work with your team to create and edit a Sway together.

- **How It Works:**
    - Share your Sway with edit permissions via a link or email.

Pro Tip: Use Microsoft Teams to coordinate feedback and edits in real time.

Example: Sarah and her colleague collaborated on a product launch Sway, ensuring it met their team's expectations.

Example: Sarah used Copilot to rephrase her project description, making it more concise and impactful.

These tips and tricks will help you maximize Sway's potential, enabling you to create presentations that are as engaging as they are professional.

COMMON PITFALLS AND HOW TO AVOID THEM

Microsoft Sway is a user-friendly and powerful tool, but like any software, missteps in its use can detract from your message and audience engagement. Understanding these common pitfalls and learning how to avoid them will help you create polished, effective Sway presentations that shine every time.

In this chapter, we'll explore frequent mistakes users encounter and provide actionable strategies to ensure your Sway projects are clear, engaging, and professional.

1. Overloading with Content

The Pitfall:
Cramming too much text, images, or multimedia into a single Sway can overwhelm your audience and dilute your message.

Why It Happens:
Sway's flexibility makes it tempting to include every detail or visual you have.

How to Avoid It:

- Focus on your main points and keep supporting content concise.
- Use headings and sections to organize your content into digestible chunks.
- Limit visuals to those that directly support or enhance your narrative.

Example: Sarah initially cluttered her Sway with dozens of images from a product launch event. After removing redundant visuals and focusing on key moments, her presentation became much more impactful.

Pro Tip: Preview your Sway to see how it flows and adjust accordingly.

2. Ignoring Audience Needs

The Pitfall:
Creating a Sway that doesn't align with the interests or technical abilities of your audience.

Why It Happens:
Failing to consider the audience's perspective during the planning stage.

How to Avoid It:

- Identify your audience's expectations, technical comfort level, and preferred presentation style.

- Use navigation and content appropriate for their needs (e.g., simple layouts for less tech-savvy viewers).

Example: Sarah tailored her Sway for a client presentation by using a professional tone, concise text, and clear visuals instead of relying on heavy multimedia.

Pro Tip: Conduct a quick survey or ask for feedback from a small group before finalizing your Sway.

3. Poor Use of Navigation Options

The Pitfall:
Choosing a navigation style that doesn't complement your content or audience.

Why It Happens:
Defaulting to a single navigation option without considering alternatives.

How to Avoid It:

- Choose vertical scrolling for detailed reports or timelines.

- Opt for horizontal scrolling for visually driven narratives.

- Use slide navigation for structured presentations or lectures.

Example: Sarah initially used horizontal scrolling for a data-heavy report, which confused her audience. Switching to vertical scrolling made the content easier to follow.

Pro Tip: Test multiple navigation styles during the design phase to find the best fit.

4. Overusing Interactive Elements

The Pitfall:
Adding too many interactive features like embedded videos, polls, or animations can distract your audience.

Why It Happens:
The excitement of Sway's interactivity features can lead to overuse.

How to Avoid It:

- Use interactive elements sparingly and only when they enhance your message.
- Test your Sway to ensure interactive features don't disrupt the flow or load times.

Example: Sarah removed a redundant quiz from her Sway, focusing instead on a single, impactful video.

Pro Tip: Ask yourself if an interactive element adds value or if it's just filler.

5. Inconsistent Design Choices

The Pitfall:
Mixing too many colors, fonts, or themes can make your Sway look unprofessional and hard to read.

Why It Happens:
Experimenting with design options without a cohesive plan.

How to Avoid It:

- Stick to a consistent color palette, font style, and theme throughout your Sway.

- Use Sway's built-in design engine or themes to maintain visual harmony.

Example: Sarah initially used multiple fonts and clashing colors in her Sway. By sticking to her company's branding guidelines, she created a cohesive and professional look.

Pro Tip: Use the "Preview" function frequently to assess overall design consistency.

6. Neglecting Accessibility

The Pitfall:
Failing to make your Sway accessible to all viewers, including those with disabilities.

Why It Happens:
Overlooking accessibility features or not considering diverse audience needs.

How to Avoid It:
- Use high-contrast themes for better visibility.

- Add alternative text (alt text) to all images and media.

- Test navigation and readability with screen readers.

Example: Sarah added alt text to her visuals, ensuring her presentation was accessible to visually impaired viewers.

Pro Tip: Use Microsoft's accessibility checker to identify and fix issues in your Sway.

7. Ignoring Mobile Compatibility

The Pitfall:
Designing a Sway that looks great on a desktop but is difficult to navigate on smaller screens.

Why It Happens:
Not testing the presentation on multiple devices.

How to Avoid It:

- Preview your Sway on desktops, tablets, and smartphones.

- Adjust text size and image placement for mobile-friendly viewing.

Example: Sarah noticed that her detailed charts were difficult to read on mobile devices. She simplified the visuals and ensured key data points were emphasized.

Pro Tip: Avoid tiny text and overly complex visuals to enhance the mobile viewing experience.

8. Failing to Optimize for Sharing

The Pitfall:
Sharing your Sway without considering how it will appear to recipients or how accessible the link is.

Why It Happens:
Skipping the sharing setup or choosing the wrong permissions.

How to Avoid It:

- Use Sway's Share options to create accessible, easy-to-use links.

- Set permissions to fit your audience (e.g., public, organization-only, or specific people).

- Test the shared link before sending it to ensure everything works as intended.

Example: Sarah initially set her Sway to "organization-only," unintentionally blocking external clients. Adjusting the permissions allowed them to access the presentation.

Pro Tip: Include a brief description or instructions alongside the link when sharing your Sway.

9. Not Reviewing Before Sharing

The Pitfall:
Sending out a Sway with errors or overlooked design flaws.

Why It Happens:
Rushing to share without a final review.

How to Avoid It:

- Preview your Sway in Play mode to catch errors and ensure a smooth flow.

- Double-check spelling, grammar, and alignment.

- Test your Sway's navigation and interactive elements.

Example: Sarah caught a typo in a key statistic during her final review, saving her from an embarrassing mistake in front of clients.

Pro Tip: Have a colleague or friend review your Sway for fresh eyes on potential issues.

By avoiding these common pitfalls, you can create Microsoft Sway presentations that are not only visually stunning but also effective in delivering your message.

SARAH'S JOURNEY WITH MICROSOFT SWAY

The soft hum of Sarah's laptop filled the quiet of her office as she stared at her project timeline. A week from now, she would present her sustainability initiative to the executive team—a presentation that could determine funding for the next fiscal year. Yet, as she scrolled through her cluttered PowerPoint slides, she felt anything but confident.

"This isn't working," she muttered, closing the presentation. The slides were dense, visually chaotic, and lacked the polished edge she needed to make an impact. Sarah needed a solution, and she needed it fast.

That evening, Sarah vented her frustrations to her colleague, Jessica, during a team call. "Have you tried Sway?" Jessica asked, leaning into her webcam.

"Sway?" Sarah replied, puzzled.

"It's part of Microsoft 365. Think PowerPoint, but smarter and easier to use," Jessica explained. "It's perfect for what you're trying to do— interactive, clean, and professional."

Intrigued, Sarah opened her browser, logged into Sway, and clicked "Create New." Within minutes, she realized Jessica was right.

Sarah began by importing the content from her existing PowerPoint slides. Sway's design engine transformed her text-heavy slides into a sleek, scrollable presentation. She quickly added headings to organize her key points: "The Problem," "Proposed Solutions," and "Expected Outcomes."

"This already looks better," she thought, marveling at how effortlessly Sway arranged her content.

Sarah explored the available themes and navigation options, ultimately settling on a horizontal scrolling layout that felt modern and dynamic.

Next, Sarah turned her attention to visuals. She used Sway's built-in Bing search to find high-quality, Creative Commons-licensed images that complemented her presentation. For her section on renewable energy, she embedded a short YouTube video showcasing solar panel installations.

She grouped related elements into stacks, creating an interactive experience for her audience. When she previewed her work, Sarah was impressed by how professional it looked without any design expertise on her part.

"This is exactly what I needed," she thought.

With her presentation nearly complete, Sarah shared a preview link with Jessica. "This is amazing," Jessica replied after reviewing the Sway. "The layout is clean, the visuals are impactful, and the navigation makes it easy to follow. Just make sure you emphasize the funding impact in your closing section."

Taking Jessica's advice, Sarah added an interactive chart to her final section, showing projected savings if her initiative was funded.

Presentation day arrived, and Sarah walked into the boardroom armed with her laptop. As she cast her Sway onto the projector screen, the horizontal navigation and interactive elements immediately grabbed the attention of the executives.

Instead of flipping through static slides, Sarah guided the room through her scrollable, immersive presentation. The embedded video and interactive chart kept the audience engaged, and the polished design made her message stand out.

By the end of her presentation, Sarah could see the enthusiasm on the faces of the executives. Her hard work—and Sway—had paid off.

As Sarah returned to her desk later that day, she felt a renewed sense of confidence. Sway hadn't just helped her create a presentation—it had transformed how she approached storytelling.

"It's not just about the tool," she thought. "It's about how it helps you connect with your audience and bring your ideas to life."

Sarah's story is a reminder that with the right tools and a bit of creativity, anyone can create presentations that inspire and engage. Whether you're presenting to executives, teaching a class, or sharing a personal story, Sway equips you with the features and flexibility to make your ideas shine.

BRINGING IT ALL TOGETHER

As we near the conclusion of this book, it's time to reflect on the journey we've taken through Microsoft Sway. From understanding its purpose to mastering its features, we've explored how Sway empowers users to create interactive, visually engaging presentations with ease. Along the way, Sarah's story has provided a relatable example of how embracing Sway can transform your approach to communication and storytelling.

1. **What Is Microsoft Sway?**
   We started by defining Sway as a modern presentation tool that combines simplicity with creativity. Its integration with Microsoft 365 and focus on interactivity make it a standout resource for users across industries.

2. **Why Use Sway?**
   We explored the benefits of Sway, from its design automation to its versatility in professional and personal projects. Whether you're a teacher, a marketer, or simply someone with a story to share, Sway offers a unique way to engage your audience.

3. **Getting Started:**
   This chapter guided you through the basics of creating your first Sway, from organizing content to choosing layouts and themes.

4. **Best Practices:**
   We covered strategies to ensure your Sway projects are clear, visually appealing, and audience-focused.

5. **Tips and Tricks:**
   Hidden features and creative techniques—like using the Remix button and embedding interactive elements—can take your Sways to the next level.

6. **Common Pitfalls:**
   We addressed frequent challenges, like overloading content and

ignoring audience needs, and provided solutions to ensure your Sways remain professional and effective.

7. **Episode: Sarah's Journey with Sway:**
   Through Sarah's experience, we saw how Sway's features come to life in a real-world context. From creating an engaging presentation to impressing her audience, Sarah's transformation demonstrated the practical power of this tool.

Sarah's story resonates because it mirrors the challenges and triumphs many of us face when working with new tools. Initially overwhelmed by the limitations of traditional presentation software, Sarah embraced Sway's innovative approach and discovered a new way to communicate her ideas.

Her journey illustrates several key lessons:

- **Simplicity Is Powerful:** By letting Sway handle design, Sarah focused on crafting her message, resulting in a more impactful presentation.

- **Interactivity Engages Audiences:** From embedded videos to dynamic layouts, Sarah's use of Sway's interactive features captured her audience's attention.

- **Tools Enhance Creativity:** Copilot and Sway's intelligent features didn't just save Sarah time—they helped her refine and elevate her work.

Sarah's journey reflects your own as you've explored Sway throughout this book. Like her, you've learned to approach presentations with fresh eyes, leveraging tools and strategies that simplify the process while amplifying your impact.

Whether you're creating a report, teaching a class, or sharing a personal story, Sway equips you to communicate more effectively. As you apply the lessons and insights from this book, you'll find yourself growing more confident and creative in your projects.

Remember: the journey doesn't stop here. Sway is part of the larger Microsoft 365 ecosystem, and mastering it opens the door to even greater possibilities. Tools like Teams, SharePoint, and OneDrive work seamlessly with Sway, creating an integrated experience that enhances every aspect of your workflow.

EMBRACING CREATIVITY AND CONNECTION

As we close this book, it's clear that Microsoft Sway is more than just a presentation tool—it's a gateway to creativity, connection, and transformation. Whether you've learned to streamline a business report, design a captivating newsletter, or share a personal story, Sway has given you the tools to communicate in ways that are impactful, engaging, and uniquely yours.

But this isn't the end of your journey. Sway is part of a dynamic and ever-evolving ecosystem of Microsoft 365 tools, each designed to help you work smarter, collaborate more effectively, and express your ideas with confidence.

Throughout this book, you've explored Sway's powerful features, from its intuitive design engine to its interactive elements and AI-powered Copilot. Each chapter has provided insights into creating polished, professional presentations with ease. More importantly, you've seen how Sway can transform the way you approach communication.

Think of the possibilities that lie ahead:

- **For Business Professionals:** Impress clients with sleek, interactive proposals.
- **For Educators:** Engage students with dynamic lesson plans and study materials.
- **For Personal Projects:** Share travel journals, event recaps, and creative endeavors that inspire.

Whatever your goals, Sway's flexibility and simplicity make it a valuable asset for anyone who has a story to tell.

Microsoft Sway doesn't exist in isolation. It's part of the robust Microsoft 365 ecosystem, designed to work seamlessly with tools like

Teams, SharePoint, OneDrive, and Word. As you've seen in this book, integrating these tools can amplify your productivity and creativity.

As you continue exploring Microsoft 365, you'll discover how these tools can complement one another, making your workflow more efficient and your projects more impactful.

Sarah's story serves as a reminder that learning is a continuous process. Like Sarah, you've taken the first steps toward mastering Sway, overcoming challenges, and discovering new possibilities. But growth doesn't stop here.

- **Experiment:** Try new features, templates, and layouts in your future Sway projects.

- **Expand Your Knowledge:** Explore other tools in the *Microsoft 365 Companion Series* to deepen your understanding of the ecosystem.

- **Stay Curious:** The world of technology evolves rapidly, and staying open to learning will keep you ahead of the curve.

Your decision to learn Sway is more than an investment in a tool—it's an investment in yourself. By embracing new technologies and refining your skills, you're not just keeping up with the modern world—you're shaping it.

This book is one step in a larger journey. As you master Sway and explore the broader Microsoft 365 suite, you'll find yourself empowered to work more effectively, collaborate more seamlessly, and share your ideas with greater impact.

Thank you for allowing this book to be part of your learning journey. Here's to continued growth, creativity, and connection. Your story is just beginning, and with Microsoft Sway, the possibilities are endless. Let's keep moving forward together!